How to Massage Your Cat

by
Jane Buckle

Illustrations by Ron Young

HOWELL
BOOK
HOUSE

For Mark and Elizabeth.

Howell Book House
MACMILLAN
A Simon & Schuster Macmillan Company
1633 Broadway
New York, NY 10019

MACMILLAN is a registered trademark of Macmillan, Inc.

Library of Congress Cataloging-in-Publication Data

Buckle, Jane.
    How to massage your cat / by Jane Buckle: illustrations
by Ron Young.
        p.   cm
    ISBN 0-87605-793-8
        1. Cats—Diseases—Alternative treatment.   2. Massage
for animals.
I. Title.
SF985.B835   1996
636.8'0895822—dc20   95-51775
                                                    CIP

Manufactured in the United States of America
10 9 8 7 6 5 4 3 2 1

Contents

Introduction

I have always been a cat lover. I like the way they are so independent. Just before I moved to London from Bath my elderly cat, Mr. Tiger, died. It was almost as though he thought, "I am too old for change, so I'll go now."

I missed him more than I thought possible.

After two catless years, I was involved in a serious car accident on Christmas Eve. My family and I miraculously survived. Over the next few days I realized I needed a cat to help my recovery. Cats are so wonderfully peaceful and soothing. My daughter and I went to the Battersea Dog Home in London (they have cats, too), where we fell in instant love with a two-year-old tabby who had been abandoned over Christmas. We adopted him on the spot and called him Mr. Sydney.

As soon as he came home with us I started our mutual therapy. Massage for me to bond to Mr. Sydney and to help me relax; massage for Mr. Sydney to help him lose his fear of humans and bond to his new home. One day while massaging him, I thought how nice it would be to share this with others. The book was born.

The Whereforalls

Chapter 1

Why Massage Your Cat?

A cat is one of the most touchy-feely animals alive.

Cats positively thrive on being stroked, and if you are already stroking your pet, why not try something a little more therapeutic? Massage is good for your cat. It improves the circulation, eases aches and pains and is as comforting to the giver as to the receiver.

In fact, massage is nature's stress management therapy. It is well known that massage reduces your pet's blood pressure and your own. So why not set aside a special time for both of you to experience the delights of strokability?

It also stops those telephonaholics in their tracks. Just murmur, "I must go, it's time for the cat's massage," and you will be rewarded with a blissful silence.

Chapter 2

When to Massage Your Cat

Well, what's wrong with starting right now?

Whisper *massage* into your cat's ear. Linger over the *s's*. Your pet will respond with a curious look until he has learned the word. But then he will roll over onto his back, smile a dreamy smile and whisper back, *me-ooh, now*.

Chapter 3

Where to Massage Your Cat

You can massage your cat almost anywhere, but it adds to a sense of routine (cats love routine) and ritual (humans love ritual) if you keep using the same place. Some folks choose their laps, some the kitchen table, some the floor. I have known cats massaged on window sills, on the draining board and on top of the dryer.

Wherever you choose, allow your pet some say in the decision. A casual stroll around your home together will usually produce a "Yep, that's the place," from your pet.

Chapter 4

With What to Massage Your Cat

Using your fingers alone to massage your cat will work just fine. However, a little cold-pressed oil—just enough to moisten your fingers—will be even better. (No, not cooking oil, that really won't do.) Cold-pressed vegetable oils like grapeseed and sweet almond can be bought at most healthfood stores.

Again, allow your pet to show her preference. Different oils have different smells, and cats are a finicky bunch. It might be a good idea to switch every once in a while.

Chapter 5

Pointers on Purring

It is important, when massaging your cat, to become aware of the different purring levels of approval:

1. The purring murmur. This means, "I am taking notice."

2. The slow, throaty purr. This means, "Yes, OK, definitely."

3. Full throttle, no-holds-barred motor mower. This means, "Don't stop!"

Number 3 is the one you are aiming for, but at this level, the vibrations can be major. Remove all nearby objects that might fall over.

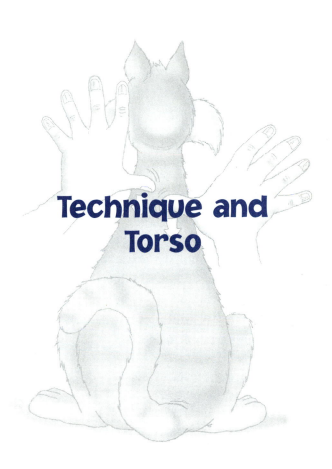

Technique and Torso

Chapter 6

Fingertip Massage

This is a gentle, slow, rhythmic walking of your fingers up and down, gently combing through your cat's fur.

Allow your first two fingers (index and the next one) to do the walking, and drag your thumbs behind so there is a roll of cat skin being gently pulled in the direction of the walking fingers. You can use one hand or both simultaneously.

Repeat this in lines up and down the body of your cat, and you will soon be rewarded with a tumultuous purr and an adoring look.

Chapter 7

Thumb Massage

This is perfect for someone who is "all thumbs."

At the neck area, and just using the sides of both thumbs on each side of the spine, push the fur in sections of about two inches, alternately, toward the tail. This will stimulate the nerve area around the spine and prove deeply satisfying to your cat. It is best attempted sitting behind your cat, with him facing away from you.

Although you need to apply fairly firm pressure, do not press too hard or your cat will edge away from you, which could upset your balance.

Chapter 8

Circle Massage

A delicious massage to do while you are daydreaming, as it has no beginning and no end. In fact, you can while away many an hour, cat and owner together, meandering along the daydream highway as you share the soothing sensations of a circling massage.

Using three fingers of both hands, gently move them in opposite directions, drawing circles. (The thumb and little finger sit this one out.) You can draw circles all over your cat, which is great fun for you both!

Chapter 9

Massage by Foot

These days we are often pressed for time, but our cats still demand attention.

Thus, the beauty of foot massage.

It can be done while you're reading, writing or watching TV. It is a good idea to keep your socks on in the process, since some cats view toes as mice that just happen to be attached to the end of your feet!

Chapter 10

Chest Massage

This could well become your cat's favorite massage.

Begin gently on his chest with the circle massage, then progress to the fingertip massage. Very gingerly, move on toward the stomach area using both thumb and finger movements.

Let me warn you, some cats instinctively react defensively to movement toward their tummies and will, most emphatically, tell you so (the scratches will heal). Should your cat show her claws, she may be attempting to reciprocate the massage, not retaliate. This is the highest form of praise.

Most cats will, however, want you to do this for hours and may object to the end of the session. For this reason, have a clock handy and set the alarm to go off at a designated time.

Chapter 11

Tail Massage

Cats are very proud of their tails. They preen them for hours and are not at all sure about having them messed up. Always take a tail massage very seriously.

Starting at the base, massage slowly toward the tip of the tail, making sure the coat lies flat. Be prepared for some tail swishing while your pet gets used to it. If you have a very large cat, do not hang on and keep breakables well clear.

Chapter 12

Back and Hindquarters Massage

Most cats love having their backs massaged. They will arch in pure pleasure and keep moving until you have found the perfect spot.

Unfortunately, this often means that their tails sometimes swish right under your nose. With a little practice, you can learn to anticipate this and lean to one side.

Be prepared for constant motion while you perform this massage. Keep it fairly intense to avoid tickling your cat.

Types of Cats

Chapter 13

Massage for Longhaired Cats

Longhaired cats spend a tremendous amount of time preening themselves (at least a third of their lives) and they really do appreciate a helping hand.

They know their coat will become glossier as the blood supply is increased by the massage you are giving them. They also know that while you are massaging them you are unlikely to be doing anything else, and they love being the center of attention.

If your cat is exceptionally longhaired, no matter how well groomed, you may discover all manner of things. . . .

Chapter 14

Massage for Long-Whiskered Cats

Make no mistake, whiskers are very important to a cat. Whiskers actually enable cats to negotiate small openings—a cat will only attempt to squeeze through somewhere bigger than the width of his whiskers.

Whiskers mean respect with a capital W. So if your pet is long-whiskered, he deserves the same treatment as a bishop.

Tall altar candles, spiritual music and a tasseled, velvet cushion will help create the right atmosphere.

Massage reverently.

Chapter 15

Massage for Short-Whiskered Cats

Short-whiskered cats dream of having long whiskers.

As you massage your cat's face, make sure you make exaggerated gestures to show you know where his dream whiskers are.

When you have got it right, your cat will begin to resemble the Cheshire Cat in *Alice's Adventures in Wonderland*, with a smile that extends a foot in each direction.

Chapter 16

Massage for Visiting Cats

This can be tricky. You don't want the visitor to stay.

On the other hand, if you get it right the cat will never want to leave. Or worse, he could inform all his friends and you could soon be besieged.

But remember, this is the perfect cat to practice on.

Chapter 17

Massage for City Cats

City cats are real cool customers. They may have nine lives, but in cities this gets extended to nearer one dozen.

City cats are more blasé about life and have heard all about massage from their friends down the block. Don't be surprised if your cat appears very disdainful while you are learning your skill.

She is expecting a professional job, so don't disappoint her. Dressing for the part will help.

Chapter 18

Massage for Hunting Cats

"A hunting we will go, meow, meow, meow."

This is the beginning of a famous feline nurs-
ery rhyme. Whether cats are stalking a bird, a
mouse, a fly or your newly painted toenails, never
laugh. Especially when shadows are involved. To
a cat, a shadow is a very real thing—like a mirror
image, but in negative.

As an entrée to the massage, you might try a
little shadowboxing with your fingers. Chasing
shadows is always fun, and what better, after
using all that energy, than a soothing massage?

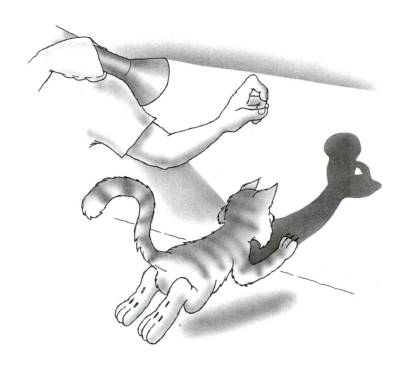

Chapter 19

Massage for Lady Cats

Diamonds may be a girl's best friend, but when it comes to our feline friends, food and touch are the passport to love....

Swap diamonds for freshly cooked fish or chicken livers, add a regular massage, and you will be rewarded by a tumultuous purr—Level 3 (see Chapter 5, "Pointers on Purring").

Diamonds may be forever, but who lives that long? Spoil your cat with gourmet food to tantalize her tastebuds. Indulge those dreams of luxury with a long, languid massage, and *you* will be rewarded by diamonds—in your pet's eyes!

Chapter 20

Massage for Pregnant Cats

Pregnant cats need more time, more love and more reassurance from their owners. After all, no ultrasound has told them how many mouths they will have to feed—or how soon! Keep telling your mother-to-be that she is *soooo* beautiful and *soooo* clever to be pregnant, and try to mean it.

Tell her not to worry about her expanding waistline while you gently massage her tummy.

Chapter 21

Massage for Kittens

A kitten is a ball of mischievous fur—a curious, innocent and utterly adorable bundle. By gently massaging this wriggling round of delight, you are laying the foundation for a long and lasting relationship.

Furthermore, you are teaching him the rudiments of good grooming. Mother Cat will be very pleased and will appreciate the extra free time.

Chapter 22

Massage for Ancient Cats

Old cats know when they are old. Just like humans, they worry about not being loved because they are no longer young, slim and full of energy. Always revere your ancient cats. They are full of wisdom, which they will impart to you with long, silent conversations while you help them by massaging their aching limbs.

Stare into the eyes of an ancient cat while gently massaging his hindquarters, and be prepared to receive the wisdom of centuries of cat intuition.

Your life will never be the same.

Chapter 23

Massage for Mousers

Perhaps the highest accolade your cat can bestow on you is a dead mouse. These gifts are frequently delivered to you at the most inconvenient moments or in the most inappropriate places—like in the middle of that special dinner.

Do not spoil this delicate act of love, but reward your pet with a spontaneous massage. This will remove all thoughts of further mousing from his brain. The dead mouse you can secretly replace later with a toy one.

Chapter 24

Massage for Pedigrees

Pedigreed cats, like Persians and Siamese, are exotic and they know it. Legend has it the Siamese are reincarnated from the kings and queens of Thailand, so obviously they expect the best things in life, preferably on a silver platter.

When it comes to massage, pedigreed cats presume you will deliver the very best. Why not invest in a cat massage table, covered with the softest terry toweling, and indulge them in an extremely royal way?

Cats with Quirks

Chapter 25

Massage for Cats Who Knead

Cats who knead are just telling you how much they need you. It is their own special way of showing appreciation, and is usually demonstrated when you are wearing expensive—and delicate—clothes.

The way around this is to explain to your pet when you are about to get all dressed up. Massage him as you explain.

Then tell him firmly that kneading your Oscar de la Renta's is not a good way to enhance your relationship. He will get the message—eventually.

Chapter 26

Massage for Cats Who Sit on Your Head

These cats are desperate for attention and want the whole world at their feet. A lengthy, luxurious massage is just what they need to put everything in perspective.

First, gently remove the cat from your head. If she digs her claws in, it is perfectly possible to give the massage *in situ*. If you do this, it might help to use a mirror so you can watch exactly which part of the cat you're massaging.

Chapter 27

Massage for Cats Who Climb Trees

It is obvious, really, when you stop to think about it: These cats love—and need—height. So indulge some of their fantasies. Try massaging them on the top of a stepladder, or on the garage roof. Not only will your cat be duly impressed, but you will see your life from a whole new perspective!

Chapter 28

Massage for Cats Who Sit on Your Keyboard

If your cat insists on climbing on your piano keyboard, be creative and massage him right there.

If music is the food of love, what a duet you'll play!

Chapter 29

Massage for Jealous Cats

Hell hath no fury like a cat scorned, and don't we know it?! Whether caused by a new baby, a visitor or an exciting book, we get the hostile back profile, and all our plaintive pleas are ignored.

There is only one thing to do: Massage this furry feline fury until she melts into meows of momentous pleasure. Just show a jealous cat how much you care and she will be transformed. Cinderella will go to the ball!

Chapter 30

Massage for Wandering Cats

Some cats are born with a wandering heart. You need to understand this and give your pet time out—and that means no cross owner waiting up.

Before he goes out, give him a special short massage just to show you know he will be coming home to you. Then, when he has gone, put out a saucer of milk and a few extra nibbles to welcome home the wanderer.

Your loved one will be back before breakfast, hungry, tired and oh-so-happy not to be nagged.

Chapter 31

Massage for Would-Be Tigers

Remember the dignity of a cat. He believes he is a tiger even if you don't.

Never embarrass this kind of cat; he will take a long time to forgive you. Just remember that, although your pussycat might be firmly convinced he is a 150-pound tiger, a gentle approach can turn any 150-pound tiger into a pussycat.

For this reason, when you have finished your massage, always make sure his coat is lying flat and smooth. After all, you never know who might drop in, and a tiger-cat knows he must always be prepared.

Chapter 32

Massage for Cats Who Sometimes Smell

Cats, just like humans, can feel out of sorts occasionally. This can present itself as a slight odor. A cat in good condition will not have an odor. If your cat begins to smell, make sure to check her teeth and diet with your veterinarian. But a little gentle massage may help her feel *less* out of sorts.

If, however, she has rolled or stepped in something *really* smelly, a bath might be in order.

Chapter 33

Massage for Cats with Hairballs

Hairballs can often be a real problem for cats. They are caused by ingesting hair during the preening process. Some cats can expel them naturally, and you would never notice. But some require medication and lots of TLC.

For these cats, use gentle fingertip massage between hips and ribs. (If you feel a substantial blockage, take your pet to see your vet.) Massage also helps by removing excess hair and improving the digestive process. Do not stand in the line of fire.

Beyond the Basics

Chapter 34

Massage by Disabled Owners

Cats don't bark. Cats don't need to be walked; they are perfectly happy with a tray of kitty litter. The three things a cat craves are warmth, food and love. These are easily supplied by most disabled owners.

In return you will be given a furry companion who is rarely bored and is happy to sit with you for hours, provided you give him frequent massages and cuddles.

Cats make such great companions; they fulfill so many needs (although few have been known to push a wheelchair).

Chapter 35

Massage on Vacation

Vacation is a time for special treats and special massages. And for being together.

Letters . . .

Chapter 36

Letters from Satisfied Cats

From Angelina, the Persian:

I am so pleased my mistress read your book. You really know what goes on in a cat's heart and mind. Whereas before I used to be lucky if I had an occasional stroke, now I have this delicious thing called massage twice a day. Not only does it feel good, but my mistress goes all gooey-eyed and is much easier to live with. Thank you so much.

From Sebastian, the black-and-white fluffy:

My master was given your book as a housewarming gift. It sat on the bedside table unread until his young niece came to stay one weekend. She picked it up after bringing him his supper one night (he is disabled) and laughed so hard, my master begged her to read it to him. Now he gives me a wonderful massage every day. He is especially good at the fingertip massage. He is really pleased with his new skill, and so am I!

From **Pretzel,** the longhaired Tabby:

I live with two other cats on a farm way out in the country. We work hard keeping the mice at bay and never got much stroking—that is until the family was given your book! Now whenever Tom goes out he receives a massage. When Daisy gets stuck up a tree she gets a massage, and when I forget to preen myself, someone gives me a massage for longhaired cats. Our farm has never been happier. Thank you so much.

From **Hookie,** the (former) shelter kitten:

I am the luckiest kitty alive. I was living in a small space with metal bars in front and lots of other crying cats around until the human of my dreams reached in and started petting me in a very special way. She lifted me into her arms and before I knew it I was in a big house with toys all my own! I heard her say "Massage" as we were leaving The Other Place. I don't know what it means, but I'm in love.

Chapter 37

Letters from Satisfied Owners

Dear Jane,

I must congratulate you on your informative but very funny book. You present important information in an enjoyable way, and your little book could well change many a human/cat relationship. Well done.

A veterinarian.

Dear Jane,

My daughter gave me your book. I laughed so much, my husband actually stopped watching baseball to ask me what was so funny! I have tried the strokes on Lucy, our four-year-old tabby, and do you know, she is in seventh heaven. It took her a little while to get used to the hindquarters massage, but now I just whisper massage, as you suggested, rolling the "s," and Lucy immediately rolls onto her back, paws in the air. If I knew I wasn't being silly I would swear she murmurs "Yes, please" back. My husband keeps asking when it is going to be his turn! Best wishes.

Mrs. R. Walters

Dear Jane,

I must admit I was a complete skeptic and thought massaging anything was a bit stupid. Anyhow, I bought your book out of curiosity and read it when noone was looking. An amazing thing happened. My cat Whiskey jumped into my lap, I started giving him a circle massage, and he went into a trance of pleasure. Massaging Whiskey makes me smile. People keep telling me I am looking so much younger. It *is* crazy, but it works!

    Dan P.

Dear Jane,

Your book brought two gifts to our household. The first is the gift of special touch. I always loved stroking Ebenezar, and noticed he was especially fond of having parts of his face rubbed. Now I even massage his whiskers! The second is the gift of strokability. Now that I'm using a few drops of almond oil on my fingers—and Ebie's Coat—there's much less static in his fur. It's so much nicer! Thanks, Jane.

    Eb and Lou

. . . And Your Just Reward

If you have been practicing, you should now be rewarded with a pleasured and possibly permanently purring pussycat. Continue and you may be rewarded with a gentle shoulder massage from your pet. You may not be able to "teach an old dog new tricks," but nobody said anything about cats....